Name: ______________________________

PRIMARY COPYWORK notebook

Primary Lined Paper for Copywork

SOURCE

SOURCE

SOURCE

SOURCE

SOURCE

SOURCE

SOURCE

SOURCE

/ /

SOURCE

SOURCE

SOURCE

SOURCE

/ /

SOURCE

SOURCE

/ /

SOURCE

SOURCE

/ /

/ /

SOURCE

SOURCE

/ /

SOURCE

SOURCE

SOURCE

SOURCE

SOURCE

SOURCE

/ /

SOURCE

SOURCE

/ /

SOURCE

SOURCE

SOURCE

SOURCE

/ /

SOURCE

SOURCE

/ /

SOURCE

SOURCE

SOURCE

SOURCE

SOURCE

SOURCE

SOURCE

SOURCE

/ /

SOURCE

SOURCE

SOURCE

SOURCE

/ /

SOURCE

SOURCE

/ /

/ /

SOURCE

SOURCE

SOURCE

SOURCE

/ /

SOURCE

SOURCE

SOURCE

SOURCE

/ /

/ /

SOURCE

SOURCE

SOURCE

SOURCE

/ /

SOURCE

SOURCE

SOURCE

SOURCE

/ /

SOURCE

SOURCE

/ /

SOURCE

SOURCE

/ /

SOURCE

SOURCE

SOURCE

SOURCE

/ /

SOURCE

SOURCE

/ /

SOURCE

SOURCE

SOURCE

SOURCE

SOURCE

SOURCE

SOURCE

SOURCE

SOURCE

SOURCE

SOURCE

SOURCE

SOURCE

SOURCE

/ /

SOURCE

SOURCE

/ /

SOURCE

SOURCE

/ /

SOURCE

SOURCE

SOURCE

SOURCE

SOURCE

SOURCE

/ /

/ /

SOURCE

SOURCE

SOURCE

SOURCE

SOURCE

SOURCE

SOURCE

SOURCE

/ /

SOURCE

SOURCE

/ /

SOURCE

SOURCE

SOURCE

SOURCE

SOURCE

SOURCE

/ /

SOURCE

SOURCE

SOURCE

SOURCE

/ /

SOURCE

SOURCE

SOURCE

SOURCE

SOURCE

SOURCE

/ /

SOURCE

SOURCE

SOURCE

SOURCE

SOURCE

SOURCE

SOURCE

SOURCE

SOURCE

SOURCE

SOURCE

SOURCE

/ /

SOURCE

SOURCE

/ /

SOURCE

SOURCE

SOURCE

SOURCE

/ /

SOURCE

SOURCE

SOURCE

SOURCE

/ /

SOURCE

SOURCE

/ /

SOURCE

SOURCE

/ /

SOURCE

SOURCE

SOURCE

SOURCE

/ /

SOURCE

SOURCE

SOURCE

SOURCE

/ /

SOURCE

SOURCE

SOURCE

SOURCE

/ /

SOURCE

SOURCE

/ /

SOURCE

SOURCE

/ /

SOURCE

SOURCE

/ /

SOURCE

SOURCE

/ /

/ /

SOURCE

SOURCE

SOURCE

SOURCE

SOURCE

SOURCE

/ /

SOURCE

SOURCE

/ /

SOURCE

SOURCE

/ /

SOURCE

SOURCE

SOURCE

SOURCE

/ /

SOURCE

SOURCE

SOURCE

SOURCE

SOURCE

SOURCE

SOURCE

SOURCE

/ /

SOURCE

SOURCE

SOURCE

SOURCE

SOURCE

Thank you for purchasing a schoolnest notebook!

You can find a rainbow of notebook options in many school subjects (math, spelling, history timeline, science, grade level composition books, journals, and more) on:

theschoolnest.com!

Follow along on Instagram @schoolnest

Made in the USA
Columbia, SC
31 July 2023